The Art of Wealth

A Minimalist's Guide to Financial Freedom

Introduction to Minimalism

<u>What is Minimalism?</u>

Minimalism is a lifestyle philosophy that focuses on the essentials and advocates for a simplified, intentional approach to living. At its core, minimalism is about finding contentment in what truly matters and letting go of the unnecessary distractions that consume our time, energy, and resources. Minimalism has gained popularity in recent years as people have become more mindful of their consumption habits and seek to live a more sustainable, purposeful life.

The term "minimalism" has its roots in the art world. In the 1960s, artists began creating works that used a limited palette of colors, simple shapes, and clean lines. These works were seen as a reaction against the complexity and excess of the previous art movements, and they aimed to distill art down to its most basic elements. The minimalist aesthetic soon spread beyond art and into design, architecture, and other areas of life.

In the context of lifestyle, minimalism is often associated with decluttering, downsizing, and simplifying one's possessions. However, minimalism goes beyond just physical belongings. It can also refer to simplifying one's schedule, relationships, and even thoughts. By letting go of the unnecessary, we create space for the things that truly matter to us.

Minimalism is often contrasted with consumerism, which emphasizes the accumulation of possessions and the constant pursuit of more. In a consumerist society, we are bombarded with messages that tell us we need to buy more to be happy, successful, or fulfilled. Minimalism challenges these messages and encourages us to question our assumptions about what we truly need.

At its core, minimalism is about finding freedom. By letting go of the excess, we free ourselves from the burden of maintaining and acquiring more things. We also free ourselves from the pressure to conform to societal expectations and create space for the things that truly matter to us, whether that be family, creativity, travel, or something else entirely.

Minimalism is not a one-size-fits-all solution. It looks different for everyone, and it can be practiced in varying degrees. Some people may choose to live in a tiny house and own only a handful of possessions, while others may simply declutter their closets and simplify their schedules. What is important is that we are intentional about our choices and strive to live in a way that aligns with our values and priorities.

In the next chapter, we will explore how minimalism and wealth intersect and how adopting a minimalist mindset can help us achieve financial freedom.

How Minimalism and Wealth Intersect

The intersection of minimalism and wealth may seem counterintuitive at first glance. After all, the stereotypical image of a wealthy person often involves opulence, excess, and conspicuous consumption. However, minimalism and wealth are not mutually exclusive. In fact, adopting a minimalist mindset can be a powerful tool for achieving financial freedom and creating lasting wealth.

One of the key principles of minimalism is living below your means. By simplifying your life and focusing on the essentials, you can reduce your expenses and free up more of your income for saving and investing. This is especially important for those who are just starting out on their wealth-building journey. When you are able to live below your means, you can build a strong financial foundation and set yourself up for long-term success.

Minimalism also encourages us to be intentional with our spending. Instead of mindlessly buying more and more things, we are encouraged to carefully consider our purchases and only buy what we truly need or value. This can help us avoid falling into the trap of consumerism and overspending, which can quickly derail our financial goals.

Another way that minimalism and wealth intersect is through the concept of value. Minimalism encourages us to focus on the things that bring us true value and happiness, rather than chasing after the latest trends or trying to keep up with the Joneses. When we are clear on what truly matters to us, we can invest our time, money, and energy into those things and create a more fulfilling life.

Minimalism also teaches us to be mindful of our possessions and to value experiences over things. Instead of accumulating more and more possessions, we can focus on creating memorable experiences and building meaningful relationships. This can help us create a more fulfilling life while also reducing our expenses and freeing up more of our resources for saving and investing.

Finally, minimalism can help us cultivate a long-term perspective on wealth-building. By focusing on the essentials and avoiding the distractions of consumer culture, we can stay focused on our goals and make decisions that align with our long-term vision. This can help us avoid short-term thinking and impulsive decisions that can derail our financial progress.

Benefits of Minimalist Lifestyle

Minimalism is a lifestyle that emphasizes simplicity, intentionality, and mindfulness. By focusing on the essentials and letting go of the unnecessary, minimalism offers a wide range of benefits for both our physical and mental well-being. In this chapter, we will explore some of the many benefits of adopting a minimalist lifestyle.

1. Reduced Stress and Anxiety

One of the most significant benefits of minimalism is reduced stress and anxiety. When we are surrounded by clutter and excess, it can be overwhelming and distracting. By simplifying our possessions and living space, we create a more calming environment that promotes relaxation and reduces stress.

2. Increased Focus and Productivity

Minimalism also promotes increased focus and productivity. When we are surrounded by fewer distractions and have a clear sense of what is important to us, we can more easily prioritize our time and energy. This allows us to be more productive and efficient in our work and personal lives.

3. Greater Financial Freedom

As discussed earlier, minimalism can also lead to greater financial freedom. By reducing our expenses and living below our means, we can free up more of our income for saving and investing. This can help us achieve our financial goals and create a more secure future for ourselves and our families.

4. Improved Relationships

Minimalism can also improve our relationships with others. When we are intentional about our possessions and time, we can more easily focus on building meaningful connections with the people in our lives. This can help us create stronger, more fulfilling relationships with our family, friends, and community.

5. Environmental Sustainability

Another benefit of minimalism is environmental sustainability. By consuming less and focusing on the essentials, we can reduce our impact on the planet and promote a more sustainable way of living. This can include reducing our carbon footprint, using fewer resources, and supporting ethical and sustainable practices.

6. Increased Creativity

Minimalism can also lead to increased creativity. When we are not overwhelmed by clutter and excess, we can more easily focus on creative pursuits and allow our minds to wander. This can help us tap into our creativity and develop new ideas and insights.

7. Improved Health and Well-Being

Finally, minimalism can improve our overall health and well-being. By reducing stress, increasing focus and productivity, and promoting sustainable living, we can create a more balanced, healthy lifestyle that supports our physical, mental, and emotional health.

In summary, the benefits of minimalism are numerous and varied. By adopting a minimalist lifestyle, we can reduce stress and anxiety, increase focus and productivity, achieve greater financial freedom, improve our relationships, support environmental sustainability, increase creativity, and improve our overall health and well-being.

Understanding Wealth

<u>Defining Wealth</u>

The term "wealth" is often associated with material possessions, such as money, property, and luxury goods. While these may be indicators of wealth, they do not fully encompass the meaning of the term. In this chapter, we will explore the various definitions of wealth and what it means to be truly wealthy.

1. Material Wealth

The most commonly recognized form of wealth is material wealth, which refers to the possession of physical assets such as money, property, and possessions. Material wealth is often equated with financial success, and those who possess significant amounts of material wealth are often considered wealthy. However, material wealth alone does not necessarily lead to happiness or fulfillment.

2. Human Capital

Another form of wealth is human capital, which refers to the knowledge, skills, and abilities of an individual. This includes education, experience, and personal attributes such as creativity, resilience, and emotional intelligence. Human capital is a valuable asset that can lead to financial success and personal fulfillment.

3. Social Capital

Social capital refers to the network of relationships and connections an individual has with others. This includes friends, family, colleagues, and community members. Social capital can provide access to resources, opportunities, and support, and is an essential aspect of personal and professional success.

4. Time Wealth

Time wealth refers to the freedom to use one's time as they choose. This includes having the flexibility to pursue personal interests, spend time with loved ones, and engage in activities that promote health and well-being. Time wealth is often associated with financial freedom, as it allows individuals to prioritize their time over work and career.

5. Spiritual Wealth

Finally, spiritual wealth refers to a sense of purpose, meaning, and fulfillment in life. This may include a connection to a higher power, a sense of inner peace, or a feeling of alignment with one's values and beliefs. Spiritual wealth is an important aspect of overall well-being and can contribute to a sense of happiness and contentment.

The Psychology of Wealth

The acquisition of wealth is not only a matter of financial planning and investment strategies. Wealth is also intimately connected to an individual's psychology and mindset. In this chapter, we will explore the various psychological factors that influence wealth accumulation, management, and happiness.

1. Mindset and Beliefs

One of the most significant psychological factors that impact wealth is an individual's mindset and beliefs about money. Some people have a scarcity mindset, where they believe that money is scarce, and they must hold onto it tightly. Others have an abundance mindset, where they believe that money is abundant and there are always opportunities to make more. The mindset and beliefs that an individual holds about money can impact their willingness to take risks, invest in themselves, and pursue opportunities.

2. Self-Efficacy

Self-efficacy refers to an individual's belief in their ability to achieve their goals and accomplish tasks. People with high self-efficacy are more likely to take action towards their goals and persist through challenges. In the context of wealth, individuals with high self-efficacy are more likely to take risks, invest in themselves, and pursue opportunities for financial gain.

3. Delayed Gratification

Delayed gratification refers to an individual's ability to resist immediate rewards in favor of long-term goals. People who are able to delay gratification are more likely to save money, invest in their future, and resist impulse purchases that may harm their financial well-being.

4. Money Attitudes

Money attitudes refer to an individual's overall feelings and beliefs about money. This includes attitudes towards spending, saving, investing, and debt. For example, some people may view debt as a necessary evil, while others view it as a burden that should be avoided at all costs. Money attitudes can impact an individual's financial decisions, including how much money they save, how much debt they take on, and how much they are willing to invest.

5. Financial Literacy

Financial literacy refers to an individual's knowledge and understanding of financial concepts, such as budgeting, investing, and debt management. People with high levels of financial literacy are better equipped to make informed financial decisions and manage their wealth effectively.

In summary, wealth accumulation and management are not only about financial planning and investment strategies. The psychology of wealth plays an important role in an individual's ability to build and manage wealth effectively. Factors such as mindset and beliefs, self-efficacy, delayed gratification, money attitudes, and financial literacy all impact an individual's financial decisions and overall well-being.

Building a Wealth Mindset

<u>Mindset and Wealth</u>

As we explored in the previous chapter, an individual's mindset and beliefs about money play a critical role in wealth accumulation and management. In this chapter, we will dive deeper into the different mindsets that individuals can adopt to foster wealth creation and financial abundance.

1. Abundance Mindset

An abundance mindset is one where an individual believes that wealth and opportunities for financial gain are abundant and available. This mindset focuses on the potential for growth and sees setbacks as temporary and opportunities to learn. People with an abundance mindset are more likely to take risks, invest in themselves, and pursue opportunities for financial gain.

2. Scarcity Mindset

A scarcity mindset is one where an individual believes that wealth and opportunities for financial gain are scarce and limited. This mindset focuses on lack and limitations and often leads to a fear of loss or failure. People with a scarcity mindset are more likely to hold onto their money tightly, avoid risks, and miss out on opportunities for financial growth.

3. Growth Mindset

A growth mindset is one where an individual believes that their abilities and potential can be developed through hard work and dedication. This mindset sees setbacks as opportunities for growth and focuses on continuous learning and improvement. People with a growth mindset are more likely to take calculated risks, invest in themselves, and pursue opportunities for financial growth.

4. Fixed Mindset

A fixed mindset is one where an individual believes that their abilities and potential are fixed and cannot be developed or improved. This mindset sees setbacks as evidence of inherent limitations and often leads to a fear of failure or rejection. People with a fixed mindset are more likely to avoid risks, shy away from challenges, and miss out on opportunities for financial growth.

5. Gratitude Mindset

A gratitude mindset is one where an individual focuses on the positives in their life and appreciates the abundance that they have. This mindset sees wealth and financial abundance as a blessing and an opportunity to give back and make a positive impact in the world. People with a gratitude mindset are more likely to give back, invest in causes they care about, and feel a sense of fulfillment and purpose in their financial pursuits.

In summary, an individual's mindset and beliefs about money play a critical role in their ability to build and manage wealth effectively. The different mindsets that individuals can adopt - abundance, scarcity, growth, fixed, and gratitude - all have unique impacts on financial decision-making and overall well-being. By cultivating a positive and growth-oriented mindset towards wealth, individuals can create a foundation for financial success and abundance in their lives.

Overcoming Limiting Beliefs

Limiting beliefs are beliefs that individuals hold about themselves or the world around them that limit their potential for growth and success. These beliefs often stem from past experiences, societal conditioning, or negative self-talk, and can significantly impact an individual's ability to accumulate wealth and achieve financial success. In this chapter, we will explore strategies for identifying and overcoming limiting beliefs that may be holding you back from financial abundance.

1. Recognize and Challenge Your Limiting Beliefs

The first step in overcoming limiting beliefs is to recognize them and challenge them. This involves identifying the thoughts and beliefs that may be holding you back from achieving your financial goals and questioning their validity. Ask yourself questions such as "Is this belief based on fact or assumption?" or "What evidence do I have that supports or contradicts this belief?" Challenging your limiting beliefs can help you gain a more realistic perspective and develop a more positive and empowering mindset towards wealth.

2. Reframe Your Beliefs

Reframing your beliefs involves taking a negative or limiting belief and transforming it into a positive and empowering one. For example, if you believe that "money is the root of all evil," you can reframe this belief to "money is a tool that can be used for good or bad, and I choose to use it for good." Reframing your beliefs can help you shift your mindset towards abundance and develop a more positive relationship with money.

3. Practice Gratitude

Gratitude is a powerful tool for overcoming limiting beliefs and fostering a positive mindset towards wealth. By focusing on what you already have and expressing gratitude for it, you can shift your attention away from what you lack and develop a more abundant mindset. Try starting a gratitude journal or incorporating a gratitude practice into your daily routine to cultivate a more positive and grateful attitude towards wealth.

4. Seek Support

Overcoming limiting beliefs can be challenging, and it can be helpful to seek support from others who have gone through similar experiences. Consider joining a support group or working with a coach or therapist who specializes in helping individuals overcome limiting beliefs. Surrounding yourself with positive and supportive people can help you stay motivated and on track towards achieving your financial goals.

5. Take Action

Finally, taking action is crucial for overcoming limiting beliefs and achieving financial success. Identify small steps that you can take towards your financial goals, and commit to taking action even if it feels uncomfortable or scary. By taking action, you can build momentum and confidence, and develop a more positive and empowering mindset towards wealth.

Developing a Growth Mindset

A growth mindset is the belief that intelligence, abilities, and talents can be developed and improved through dedication, hard work, and persistence. This mindset is in contrast to a fixed mindset, which is the belief that intelligence and abilities are fixed and cannot be changed. Developing a growth mindset is essential for achieving financial success, as it allows individuals to embrace challenges, persist through obstacles, and learn from failure. In this chapter, we will explore strategies for developing a growth mindset and cultivating a more positive and empowering attitude towards wealth.

1. Embrace Challenges

One of the key aspects of developing a growth mindset is embracing challenges. Instead of avoiding challenges or giving up when faced with difficulty, individuals with a growth mindset see challenges as opportunities for growth and learning. They are willing to take risks, try new things, and persist through obstacles, even when the outcome is uncertain. By embracing challenges, individuals can develop resilience, persistence, and a more positive attitude towards wealth.

2. Learn from Failure

Another important aspect of a growth mindset is the ability to learn from failure. Instead of seeing failure as a personal deficiency or a sign of inadequacy, individuals with a growth mindset view failure as an opportunity to learn and grow. They are willing to take risks, try new things, and accept the possibility of failure as part of the learning process. By learning from failure, individuals can develop resilience, adaptability, and a more positive attitude towards wealth.

3. Cultivate a Love for Learning

A growth mindset is also characterized by a love for learning. Individuals with a growth mindset are curious, open-minded, and eager to learn new things. They seek out new experiences, ask questions, and actively seek feedback to improve their performance. By cultivating a love for learning, individuals can develop a more positive and empowering attitude towards wealth, as they view education and personal development as essential for success.

4. Focus on Effort and Process

In a growth mindset, the focus is on effort and process rather than innate ability or talent. Individuals with a growth mindset believe that hard work, persistence, and dedication are more important than natural talent or intelligence. They set goals, develop a plan, and work diligently towards achieving their objectives, even when progress is slow or difficult. By focusing on effort and process, individuals can develop a more positive and empowering attitude towards wealth, as they recognize that success is the result of consistent effort and dedication.

5. Seek Feedback and Support

Finally, seeking feedback and support is essential for developing a growth mindset. By seeking feedback, individuals can gain valuable insights into their strengths and weaknesses, and identify areas for improvement. Similarly, seeking support from others can provide encouragement, motivation, and accountability, which can be essential for developing a more positive and empowering attitude towards wealth.

In conclusion, developing a growth mindset is essential for achieving financial success and cultivating a positive and empowering attitude towards wealth. By embracing challenges, learning from failure, cultivating a love for learning, focusing on effort and process, and seeking feedback and support, individuals can develop the resilience, persistence, and positive attitude necessary to achieve their financial goals. With a growth mindset, individuals can overcome obstacles, persist through challenges, and achieve their full potential, both financially and personally.

Living Below Your Means

<u>Importance of frugality</u>

Frugality is the habit of being economical and avoiding waste. It is often associated with living a simple lifestyle, but it can be a powerful tool for accumulating wealth. Frugality allows individuals to be intentional with their spending and to prioritize their long-term financial goals over short-term gratification.

One of the key benefits of frugality is that it enables individuals to live below their means. This means that they are spending less than they earn, which is essential for building wealth. By being mindful of their spending and avoiding unnecessary expenses, individuals can free up money that can be used to invest or save for the future.

Frugality also helps individuals to develop a sense of discipline and self-control. It requires making conscious choices about what to spend money on and what to avoid. This can be challenging at times, but it can also be empowering. By learning to live on less, individuals can break free from the cycle of consumerism and find greater satisfaction in the things that truly matter to them.

In addition to these benefits, frugality can also help individuals to reduce their financial stress and increase their financial security. By having a better understanding of their expenses and financial goals, individuals can make more informed decisions about their spending and saving habits. This can lead to a greater sense of financial control and peace of mind.

Of course, frugality is not without its challenges. It requires discipline, patience, and a willingness to make sacrifices in the short-term for long-term gain. It can also be difficult to balance the desire to save money with the need to enjoy life in the present moment. However, by keeping their long-term financial goals in mind and staying focused on what truly matters to them, individuals can develop a healthy and sustainable approach to frugality that can help them achieve greater financial freedom and security.

Tips for living below your means

Living below your means is a crucial aspect of building wealth. It requires being intentional with your spending and prioritizing your long-term financial goals over short-term gratification. However, it can be challenging to know where to start or how to make the necessary changes to your lifestyle. Here are some tips for living below your means:

1. Create a budget: The first step in living below your means is to have a clear understanding of your income and expenses. Start by creating a budget that outlines all of your monthly expenses, including rent/mortgage, utilities, groceries, transportation, and any other bills. Once you have a clear picture of your expenses, you can begin to identify areas where you can cut back.
2. Identify your priorities: Living below your means does not mean sacrificing everything you enjoy. It's important to identify your priorities and allocate your resources accordingly. This might mean cutting back on certain expenses, such as dining out

or buying new clothes, in order to prioritize other areas, such as travel or hobbies.

3. Cut back on discretionary spending: Discretionary spending refers to expenses that are not essential for daily living. This might include eating out, buying new clothes or gadgets, or subscribing to entertainment services. By reducing your discretionary spending, you can free up money that can be used to invest or save for the future.

4. Find ways to save on necessities: While it's important to avoid sacrificing your quality of life, there are often ways to save money on essential expenses. For example, you might consider buying in bulk or shopping at discount stores for groceries. You might also consider using public transportation or carpooling to save on transportation costs.

5. Use cash instead of credit: Using cash instead of credit can help you stay within your budget and avoid overspending. When you have a finite amount of cash on hand, you are more likely to be mindful of your spending and make intentional choices about where to allocate your resources.

6. Seek out alternative sources of income: Living below your means can be challenging if you have a limited income. Consider seeking out alternative sources of income, such as freelance work or a side business. By diversifying your income streams, you can increase your earning potential and reduce your reliance on a single source of income.

7. Practice gratitude: Living below your means requires a shift in mindset from focusing on what you don't have to appreciating what you do have. Practice gratitude by focusing on the things in your life that bring you joy and fulfillment, rather than the things you lack. This can help you maintain a

positive outlook and stay motivated on your journey toward financial freedom.

By implementing these tips and strategies, you can begin to live below your means and prioritize your long-term financial goals over short-term gratification. Remember, it's not about sacrificing everything you enjoy, but about making intentional choices and being mindful of your spending habits. With time and discipline, you can achieve greater financial freedom and security.

Budgeting basics

Budgeting is a fundamental aspect of managing personal finances and achieving financial stability. At its core, budgeting involves creating a plan that outlines your income, expenses, and savings goals. By tracking your spending and making adjustments to your budget as necessary, you can ensure that you're living within your means and making progress towards your financial objectives.

To begin budgeting, start by identifying all of your sources of income, including your salary or wages, any freelance work, and any investment income. Next, make a list of all of your expenses, including your rent or mortgage payments, utility bills, groceries, transportation costs, and any other bills or payments you make regularly.

Once you have a clear understanding of your income and expenses, you can create a budget that allocates your income towards each expense category. One common approach is the 50/30/20 rule, which suggests allocating 50% of your income towards needs (such as housing and food), 30% towards wants (such as entertainment and travel), and 20% towards savings and debt repayment.

To stick to your budget, consider using budgeting tools or apps to track your spending and monitor your progress. You may also find it helpful to set specific financial goals, such as paying off debt or saving for a down payment on a home, to keep you motivated and focused.

Additionally, be sure to regularly review and adjust your budget as necessary. Unexpected expenses or changes in income may require you to adjust your spending or savings goals, so it's important to stay flexible and adaptable. By developing good budgeting habits, you can take control of your finances and make progress towards your long-term financial goals.

Managing Debt

<u>Understanding debt</u>

Debt is a common financial tool that allows individuals and organizations to borrow money in order to finance purchases or investments that they may not otherwise be able to afford. While debt can be a useful tool for achieving financial goals, it can also be a source of stress and financial hardship if not managed properly. In this section, we will explore what debt is, how it works, and some strategies for managing it effectively.

At its simplest, debt is an obligation to repay borrowed money over time, often with interest. This can take many forms, including credit card debt, student loans, mortgages, and car loans. When you take out a loan, you agree to make regular payments to the lender over a set period of time until the debt is fully repaid. The amount of interest you'll pay on the loan will depend on factors like your credit score, the loan amount, and the loan term.

While taking on debt can be a useful way to finance big purchases or investments, it's important to be aware of the potential risks and downsides. High levels of debt can lead to financial stress, as the burden of making regular payments can be a significant drain on your income. Additionally, carrying high levels of debt can negatively impact your credit score, making it more difficult to access credit in the future.

To manage debt effectively, it's important to be proactive and organized. One of the most effective strategies for managing debt is to create a budget that prioritizes debt repayment. This might involve consolidating multiple debts into a single payment or setting up automatic payments to ensure that you don't miss any payments. Additionally, it's important to be aware of the terms of your loans and to make sure that you're not paying more in interest than necessary. If you're struggling with debt, consider reaching out to a financial advisor or credit counselor for guidance.

Finally, it's worth noting that not all debt is created equal. Some types of debt, like mortgages or student loans, may be considered "good" debt as they can lead to long-term financial benefits like homeownership or increased earning potential. Other types of debt, like credit card debt, may be considered "bad" debt as they often come with high interest rates and few long-term benefits. By understanding the different types of debt and the potential risks and benefits of each, you can make more informed decisions about when and how to take on debt.

Strategies for managing debt

Debt can be a major hurdle on the path to wealth, but it's not necessarily an insurmountable one. With some careful planning and disciplined execution, it's possible to pay down your debts and achieve financial stability. In this chapter, we'll explore some of the key strategies for managing debt and getting your finances back on track.

1. Prioritize high-interest debt: If you have multiple debts, it's important to focus your efforts on paying down the ones with the highest interest rates first. These are the debts that are costing you the most money in the long run, so paying them off quickly can help you save a lot of money on interest charges.

2. Consider debt consolidation: If you have several high-interest debts, consolidating them into a single loan with a lower interest rate can be a smart move. This can make it easier to keep track of your payments and reduce the amount of interest you pay over time. However, be sure to do your research and make sure you understand the terms and fees associated with any consolidation loan you're considering.

3. Negotiate with creditors: If you're struggling to make your payments, don't be afraid to reach out to your creditors and ask for help. Many lenders are willing to work with borrowers to set up payment plans or offer other forms of assistance, such as temporarily reducing interest rates or waiving late fees.

4. Cut expenses and increase income: One of the most effective ways to tackle debt is to free up more money to put towards your payments. This can be done by cutting unnecessary expenses, such as eating out or buying new clothes, and finding ways to increase your income, such as taking on a side gig or asking for a raise at work.

5. Use windfalls wisely: If you receive a bonus at work, a tax refund, or some other unexpected windfall, consider using it to pay down your debts. While it can be tempting to splurge on something fun or frivolous, using the money to reduce your debt burden can put you in a better financial position over the long term.

6. Build an emergency fund: Finally, it's important to have some money set aside for emergencies, such as unexpected medical expenses or car repairs. Having an emergency fund can help you avoid going deeper

into debt when unexpected expenses arise, and can give you greater peace of mind overall.

By implementing these strategies and staying focused on your goals, you can successfully manage your debt and work towards a more secure financial future.

Paying off debt

Paying off debt can be an overwhelming and challenging process, but it is a crucial step in achieving financial freedom. Once you have a solid understanding of your debt and have implemented effective strategies for managing it, it's time to focus on paying it off.

The first step is to prioritize your debts. Start by identifying which debts have the highest interest rates and focus on paying those off first. This will save you money in the long run by reducing the amount of interest you will pay over time.

One effective strategy for paying off debt is the snowball method. With this method, you start by paying off your smallest debt first, while continuing to make minimum payments on your other debts. Once your smallest debt is paid off, you move on to the next smallest debt and continue the process until all of your debts are paid off. This strategy can be effective in providing a sense of accomplishment and momentum as you see your debts gradually decreasing.

Another strategy is the avalanche method, which involves focusing on paying off your debt with the highest interest rate first. This can save you more money in the long run by reducing the amount of interest you pay overall. However, it can also take longer to see progress, which can be discouraging for some people.

Regardless of which strategy you choose, it's important to make consistent and timely payments on your debts. Consider setting up automatic payments to ensure you never miss a payment and incur additional fees or penalties.

In addition to making payments on your debts, consider ways to increase your income and reduce your expenses. This can include finding a side job, negotiating a raise or promotion at work, or cutting back on discretionary spending.

Remember that paying off debt is a marathon, not a sprint. It can take time, dedication, and discipline, but the benefits of being debt-free are worth it. By following effective strategies and staying committed to your goals, you can achieve financial freedom and a brighter financial future.

Investing for Financial Freedom

<u>Importance of investing</u>

Investing is a critical component of building wealth, and its importance cannot be overstated. Investing can help you grow your wealth and achieve your financial goals, such as retiring comfortably, buying a home, or traveling the world. At its core, investing involves taking money you have saved and putting it to work in financial markets or other vehicles in the hopes of earning a return.

One of the primary reasons investing is so important is that it allows you to generate passive income. Passive income is money earned without actively working for it. When you invest, you are putting your money to work for you, generating income through interest, dividends, or capital appreciation. Passive income is essential because it can help you achieve financial independence and reduce your reliance on earned income.

Another critical reason why investing is important is that it can help you stay ahead of inflation. Inflation is the rate at which the general level of prices for goods and services is rising, and it reduces the purchasing power of your money over time. Investing can help you earn a return that outpaces inflation, enabling you to maintain or even increase your purchasing power over time.

Investing can also help you diversify your assets and manage risk. Diversification is the practice of spreading your money across different types of assets and investments to minimize risk. By diversifying your portfolio, you can potentially reduce the impact of market fluctuations or the poor performance of any one investment on your overall financial situation.

There are many different types of investments to choose from, including stocks, bonds, mutual funds, exchange-traded funds (ETFs), real estate, and alternative investments. Each investment vehicle has its own unique risk and return characteristics, and it is essential to understand them before making investment decisions.

It is crucial to start investing early and regularly to achieve your long-term financial goals. The power of compounding, where your investment returns earn their own returns over time, can significantly amplify your returns over the long run. Even small amounts of regular contributions can add up to significant sums of money over time.

Types of investments

When it comes to investing, there are several options available to you. Each type of investment has its own advantages and disadvantages, and the choice ultimately depends on your personal goals, risk tolerance, and financial situation. In this section, we'll explore some of the most common types of investments.

1. Stocks: Stocks represent a share of ownership in a company. By buying stocks, you become a shareholder and have the opportunity to profit if the company performs well. However, stocks can also be volatile, and the value can fluctuate dramatically based on market conditions.

2. Bonds: A bond is essentially a loan to a company or government. When you purchase a bond, you're lending money with the expectation of receiving a fixed return on your investment. Bonds are generally considered less risky than stocks, but they also offer lower potential returns.

3. Real estate: Real estate can be a valuable investment, as property values tend to increase over time. You can invest in real estate by purchasing a property outright, or by investing in real estate investment trusts (REITs), which are companies that own and manage real estate properties.

4. Mutual funds: Mutual funds are collections of stocks, bonds, and other assets managed by a professional fund manager. By investing in a mutual fund, you gain exposure to a diverse range of assets without having to research and select individual investments.

5. Exchange-traded funds (ETFs): ETFs are similar to mutual funds, but they trade on stock exchanges like individual stocks. ETFs offer low fees, diversification, and ease of trading.

6. Commodities: Commodities are physical goods, such as gold, oil, and agricultural products. Investing in commodities can be a hedge against inflation, but they can also be volatile and subject to supply and demand fluctuations.

7. Cryptocurrency: Cryptocurrency is a digital or virtual currency that uses cryptography for security. Bitcoin, Ethereum, and Dogecoin are examples of popular cryptocurrencies. While cryptocurrency has the potential for high returns, it is also highly volatile and risky.

Each type of investment has its own unique risks and potential rewards. It's important to do your research and consult with a financial advisor before making any investment decisions.

Building a diversified portfolio

Building a diversified investment portfolio is a key component of successful investing. Diversification helps to reduce risk by spreading your investments across different asset classes, industries, and geographical locations. This subchapter will explore the benefits of a diversified portfolio and provide tips on how to build one.

The Importance of Diversification: A well-diversified portfolio is one that includes a mix of asset classes such as stocks, bonds, real estate, commodities, and cash. By investing in a range of assets, you can spread your risk across different industries and geographies, reducing the impact of any single asset on your portfolio. This means that if one asset class or investment performs poorly, other investments in your portfolio can potentially offset those losses.

Diversification also helps to smooth out the ups and downs of the market. The stock market can be volatile, and investing solely in stocks can lead to significant fluctuations in your portfolio's value. By diversifying into other asset classes, you can reduce the impact of market volatility on your investments.

Tips for Building a Diversified Portfolio:

1. Determine Your Investment Goals: Your investment goals should guide the construction of your portfolio. For example, if you have a long-term investment horizon, you may be comfortable taking on more risk in your portfolio. In contrast, if you have a short-term investment horizon, you may want to focus on more conservative investments.

2. Consider Your Risk Tolerance: Understanding your risk tolerance is critical when building a diversified portfolio. Your risk tolerance will help you determine the mix of assets that is right for you. Generally, younger investors with longer time horizons may be able to tolerate more risk in their portfolios, while older investors nearing retirement may want to focus on more conservative investments.

3. Invest Across Asset Classes: A diversified portfolio should include a mix of asset classes, including stocks, bonds, real estate, commodities, and cash. Consider allocating your investments across these asset classes in a way that reflects your investment goals and risk tolerance.

4. Diversify Within Asset Classes: Within each asset class, consider investing in a variety of securities. For example, if you are investing in stocks, consider investing in stocks from different industries and sectors.

5. Rebalance Your Portfolio: Over time, your portfolio may become unbalanced as certain investments perform better than others. Regularly rebalancing your portfolio can help ensure that your investments remain diversified and aligned with your investment goals.

A well-diversified portfolio is a critical component of successful investing. By spreading your investments across different asset classes, industries, and geographies, you can reduce risk and smooth out the ups and downs of the market. When building a diversified portfolio, it is essential to consider your investment goals, risk tolerance, and asset allocation, and to regularly rebalance your investments to ensure that they remain aligned with your goals.

Passive Income Streams

What is passive income?

Passive income is a term used to describe the money earned without having to actively work for it. It is a form of income that allows you to earn money while you sleep, travel, or spend time with family and friends. The concept of passive income is becoming increasingly popular, especially among people who are looking for ways to generate income outside of their regular jobs.

Passive income can come from various sources, such as rental income, dividends, interest income, royalties, and income from businesses that require minimal involvement from the owner. The key characteristic of passive income is that it requires little or no effort to maintain once it is set up.

One of the most common sources of passive income is rental income from real estate properties. If you own a rental property, you can earn rental income each month without having to actively work for it. Another example of passive income is dividend income from stocks. If you invest in dividend-paying stocks, you can earn a steady stream of income without having to actively manage your portfolio.

Another popular source of passive income is creating and selling digital products such as e-books, courses, and software. Once you create these products, you can sell them online and earn income without having to actively work for it. You can also earn passive income from affiliate marketing, where you promote other people's products and earn a commission on each sale.

Passive income has several advantages over active income. Firstly, it provides a source of income that is not dependent on your time or effort. This means that you can earn money even when you are not actively working. Secondly, passive income can provide financial stability and security. By creating multiple streams of passive income, you can diversify your income sources and reduce your dependence on any one source of income. Finally, passive income can help you achieve financial independence by giving you the freedom to pursue your passions and interests without having to worry about earning a living.

Overall, passive income is an excellent way to supplement your active income and achieve financial independence. While it requires effort and investment to set up, the long-term benefits are worth it. With the right strategies and investments, you can create a steady stream of passive income that will provide you with financial stability and freedom.

Types of passive income

Passive income is a great way to build wealth without having to actively trade time for money. In this subchapter, we will explore the different types of passive income that you can generate.

1. Rental income: Rental income is one of the most common forms of passive income. It can come from real estate properties, such as apartments, houses, or commercial buildings. Rental income can provide a steady stream of cash flow, and it's a popular investment strategy for those who want to build long-term wealth.

2. Dividend income: Dividend income comes from owning stocks in companies that pay out dividends to shareholders. Dividends are a portion of a company's earnings that are distributed to its shareholders. Dividend stocks are often considered a stable and reliable investment option for those who are looking for passive income.

3. Interest income: Interest income is earned from lending money to others, such as through bonds, CDs, or peer-to-peer lending platforms. This type of passive income can offer a predictable return on investment.

4. Royalties: Royalties are earned by owning intellectual property, such as patents, copyrights, or trademarks. These can generate passive income by licensing them to others.

5. Affiliate marketing: Affiliate marketing is a form of online marketing where you promote other people's products or services and earn a commission for each sale. This can be a lucrative source of passive income for those who have a strong online presence and audience.

6. Online courses and e-books: Creating and selling online courses or e-books can provide a source of passive income. Once the content is created, it can be sold repeatedly without requiring ongoing work.

7. Peer-to-peer lending: Peer-to-peer lending involves lending money to individuals or businesses through online platforms. This can provide a source of passive income through the interest earned on the loans.

In summary, there are many different types of passive income that can be generated. By diversifying your sources of passive income, you can create a stable and reliable stream of income that can help you achieve financial freedom.

Creating passive income streams

Passive income is a powerful tool for achieving financial freedom and security. By generating income that doesn't require active participation on a regular basis, passive income can provide a steady stream of cash flow while allowing for more flexibility in how you spend your time. In this subchapter, we'll explore the different strategies for creating passive income streams.

One of the most popular forms of passive income is rental income. This involves purchasing property, whether it's a residential home, apartment complex, or commercial space, and renting it out to tenants. While rental income does require some management and maintenance, it can be a reliable source of income over the long-term.

Another strategy for generating passive income is through dividend-paying stocks or mutual funds. These investments pay a portion of their earnings to shareholders on a regular basis, providing a steady stream of income without requiring any ongoing effort on your part.

For those with a creative streak, there are also opportunities to earn passive income through licensing creative works or developing intellectual property. This might involve licensing a piece of software, selling stock photography or music, or creating an online course.

Affiliate marketing is another way to generate passive income, by promoting other people's products or services in exchange for a commission. This might involve creating a blog or social media account that promotes certain products, or building an email list of subscribers who are interested in a particular topic or product.

Finally, there is the option of investing in real estate investment trusts (REITs), which are companies that own and manage income-generating properties. By investing in a REIT, you can receive a portion of the profits generated by the properties they manage, without having to own any physical property yourself.

No matter what strategy you choose, creating passive income streams requires an upfront investment of time and/or money. But once you've put in the effort to get your passive income stream up and running, it can provide a reliable source of income for years to come. By diversifying your passive income streams, you can also reduce your risk and increase your overall financial stability.

Real Estate Investment

<u>Benefits of real estate investing</u>

Real estate investing has been a popular wealth-building strategy for decades, and for good reason. There are a number of benefits to investing in real estate that make it an attractive option for those seeking to build wealth.

Firstly, real estate has the potential for steady cash flow through rental income. Unlike stocks or other investments, rental properties can provide consistent monthly income in the form of rent payments. Additionally, rental income is often considered passive income, meaning that it requires less active management than other forms of income such as a traditional job or business.

Real estate can also provide a hedge against inflation. As the cost of living increases over time, so too do rental rates and the value of real estate. This means that owning property can be a way to protect your wealth from the eroding effects of inflation.

Furthermore, real estate can appreciate in value over time, allowing you to build equity in your property. With the right investment strategy and careful management, you can see significant appreciation in the value of your property, which can be leveraged for future investments or to generate more income.

In addition to providing income and appreciation, real estate also offers a number of tax benefits. For example, rental income is typically taxed at a lower rate than other forms of income, and real estate investors can take advantage of deductions for expenses such as property taxes, mortgage interest, and maintenance costs.

Real estate investing also offers a level of control and autonomy that other investment options may not. As a real estate investor, you have control over your investment decisions and the ability to make strategic choices that can impact the performance of your portfolio.

Of course, as with any investment strategy, there are risks associated with real estate investing. However, with proper research, due diligence, and a solid investment strategy, the benefits of real estate investing can outweigh the risks for many investors. Overall, real estate investing can be a powerful tool for building wealth and achieving financial freedom. Its ability to generate consistent income, appreciate in value, and provide tax benefits make it an attractive option for those seeking to diversify their investment portfolio and create long-term wealth.

Different types of real estate investments

Real estate investment is a popular choice for those looking to build their wealth over time. There are many different types of real estate investments, each with their own unique advantages and risks. In this subchapter, we will explore some of the most common types of real estate investments.

1. Residential Rental Properties: This is perhaps the most well-known and traditional type of real estate investment. It involves purchasing a property and renting it out to tenants. Residential rental properties can generate a steady income stream through rent payments, and may also appreciate in

value over time. However, managing rental properties can be time-consuming and comes with the risk of tenants damaging the property or not paying rent.

2. Commercial Real Estate: This type of investment involves purchasing a property that is used for commercial purposes, such as office space, retail space, or warehouses. Commercial properties typically have longer lease terms and higher rental rates than residential properties. However, they also require higher upfront costs and may have more complex financing options.

3. Real Estate Investment Trusts (REITs): A REIT is a company that owns and operates income-generating real estate properties, such as apartment buildings, hotels, and shopping centers. Investors can purchase shares of the REIT, which entitles them to a portion of the income generated by the properties. REITs are often considered a more passive form of real estate investment, as they do not require the same level of management as owning a property outright.

4. Real Estate Crowdfunding: This type of investment allows multiple investors to pool their money together to purchase a property. Crowdfunding platforms typically allow investors to invest smaller amounts of money than they would need to purchase a property outright. However, investors in a real estate crowdfunding project may have less control over the property and its management than they would with other types of real estate investments.

5. Real Estate Development: This involves purchasing land and developing it into a property, such as a housing development or commercial building. Real estate development requires significant upfront

capital and carries a higher level of risk than other types of real estate investments. However, it can also offer the potential for high returns if the development is successful.

Each type of real estate investment has its own advantages and risks, and it is important to do your research and consider your financial goals before choosing a type of investment.

Tips for investing in real estate

Investing in real estate can be a lucrative way to build wealth over time. However, it's important to approach real estate investing with a strategic mindset and a solid understanding of the market. Here are some tips for investing in real estate:

1. Do your research: Before investing in any property, it's important to thoroughly research the market and the property itself. This includes examining the neighborhood, analyzing local market trends, and understanding the property's history and condition. This research will help you make an informed decision about whether or not the investment is worthwhile.

2. Start small: It's often best to start with a smaller investment property, such as a single-family home or a duplex, before moving on to larger properties. This allows you to gain experience and learn the ins and outs of the market without taking on too much risk.

3. Consider the numbers: Real estate investing is all about the numbers. You need to consider the

property's cash flow, operating expenses, and potential return on investment. A good rule of thumb is to aim for a cash-on-cash return of at least 8-10% and a cap rate of at least 5-7%.

4. Don't overlook the details: Real estate investing requires attention to detail. You need to carefully analyze the property's financials, legal documents, and physical condition. It's also important to have a solid understanding of local zoning laws and building codes.

5. Network with other investors: Networking with other real estate investors can provide valuable insights and help you stay up-to-date on local market trends. Consider joining a real estate investment group or attending networking events to connect with other investors.

6. Consider hiring a property manager: If you don't have the time or expertise to manage your property, consider hiring a professional property manager. A good property manager can handle day-to-day operations, such as rent collection and maintenance, and help maximize your investment returns.

7. Have an exit strategy: Real estate investing should be a long-term strategy, but it's important to have an exit strategy in place. This could involve selling the property after a certain number of years or refinancing the property to access equity.

In summary, investing in real estate can be a great way to build wealth over time, but it requires a strategic mindset and a solid understanding of the market. By following these tips and staying informed about local market trends, you can make smart real estate investments and build a successful real estate portfolio.

Entrepreneurship

<u>Entrepreneurship and wealth</u>

Entrepreneurship can be a powerful tool for creating wealth. By starting and growing a successful business, entrepreneurs have the potential to earn significant profits and build a valuable asset that can appreciate over time. However, entrepreneurship is not without its risks and challenges. In this subchapter, we will explore the connection between entrepreneurship and wealth, including the benefits and drawbacks of starting a business, the traits and skills that are essential for success, and the strategies that entrepreneurs can use to maximize their chances of creating wealth.

Benefits of entrepreneurship

One of the primary benefits of entrepreneurship is the potential to generate significant wealth. Successful entrepreneurs can create value by identifying unmet needs in the market, developing innovative solutions, and building businesses that deliver those solutions to customers. When done well, this process can result in a profitable enterprise that generates sustainable cash flow and appreciates in value over time.

Entrepreneurship also offers a high degree of autonomy and control. By starting their own businesses, entrepreneurs are free to pursue their passions, take risks, and chart their own course. This can be incredibly fulfilling and satisfying, especially for those who value independence and creativity.

Moreover, entrepreneurship can be a source of job creation and economic growth. Small businesses account for a significant portion of job growth in many countries, and successful entrepreneurs often create employment opportunities for others. By building thriving businesses, entrepreneurs can contribute to the overall health and prosperity of their communities.

Challenges of entrepreneurship

While entrepreneurship offers many benefits, it also involves significant risks and challenges. Starting a business requires a significant amount of time, effort, and capital, and there is no guarantee of success. Many entrepreneurs experience setbacks and failures before achieving success, and even then, there is always the risk of disruption from competitors or changes in the market.

Entrepreneurship also requires a unique set of skills and traits that not everyone possesses. Successful entrepreneurs are typically highly motivated, resilient, and adaptable. They are able to identify and pursue opportunities, navigate challenges, and persevere in the face of adversity.

Strategies for successful entrepreneurship

Despite the challenges of entrepreneurship, there are strategies that aspiring entrepreneurs can use to maximize their chances of success. One key strategy is to develop a strong business plan that outlines the market opportunity, the proposed solution, the competitive landscape, and the financial projections. A well-crafted business plan can help entrepreneurs to clarify their thinking, identify potential pitfalls, and communicate their vision to investors, partners, and employees.

Another important strategy is to build a strong network of mentors, advisors, and peers who can provide guidance, support, and feedback. Entrepreneurship can be a lonely and isolating experience, and having a supportive network can make a significant difference in the success of a business.

Additionally, successful entrepreneurs are able to stay agile and adaptable in the face of changing circumstances. They are constantly learning and evolving, staying attuned to shifts in the market and the needs of their customers. By being nimble and responsive, entrepreneurs can adjust their strategies and tactics to stay ahead of the competition and continue to grow their businesses.

Starting a business

Starting a business can be a powerful way to build wealth, as successful entrepreneurs can generate significant income and create assets with long-term value. However, starting a business is not easy, and requires careful planning, execution, and management.

The first step in starting a business is to identify a market need or opportunity. This can involve conducting market research, identifying gaps in the market, or developing a unique product or service that meets an unmet need. Once a market opportunity has been identified, the next step is to develop a business plan that outlines the vision, mission, and objectives of the business, as well as the strategies for achieving these goals.

A key part of any business plan is the financial plan, which outlines the expected revenue and expenses of the business, as well as the sources of funding required to start and grow the business. Depending on the scale and complexity of the business, financing may come from personal savings, loans from friends and family, angel investors, venture capital, or crowdfunding.

Once the business plan and financial plan have been developed, the next step is to set up the legal and administrative framework for the business. This may involve registering the business with local and national government bodies, obtaining the necessary licenses and permits, and hiring employees or contractors.

With the legal and administrative framework in place, the focus turns to executing the strategies outlined in the business plan. This may involve developing and marketing the product or service, building relationships with suppliers and customers, managing cash flow, and continuously monitoring and adjusting the business strategy based on market conditions and feedback from stakeholders.

Successful entrepreneurship requires a combination of creativity, passion, hard work, and resilience. It also requires a willingness to take calculated risks and learn from failure. While not all businesses will succeed, those that do can create significant wealth for their founders and contribute to economic growth and innovation.

In summary, starting a business is a challenging but rewarding path to building wealth. It requires careful planning, execution, and management, as well as a willingness to take risks and learn from failure. With the right mindset, resources, and support, entrepreneurs can create successful businesses that generate income and assets with long-term value.

Growing a successful business

Starting a business is just the beginning. Growing a successful business requires hard work, dedication, and a solid plan. Here are some key steps to take when growing your business:

1. Define Your Target Market: In order to grow your business, you need to know who your target audience is. This includes understanding their demographics, needs, and preferences. Once you have this information, you can tailor your marketing and advertising efforts to reach and engage with them.

2. Develop a Strong Brand Identity: A strong brand identity is crucial for any business looking to grow. Your brand is what sets you apart from your competitors and makes you memorable to your customers. Make sure your brand identity is consistent across all marketing channels, including your website, social media, and advertising.

3. Focus on Customer Service: A key part of growing a successful business is ensuring that your customers are satisfied. This means providing excellent customer service, responding to feedback and complaints, and going above and beyond to meet their needs. Happy customers are more likely to refer you to their friends and family, which can help grow your business through word-of-mouth.

4. Expand Your Product or Service Offerings: One way to grow your business is to expand your product or service offerings. This can help attract new customers and retain existing ones. However,

be careful not to expand too quickly or in a direction that doesn't align with your core business.

5. Build a Strong Team: As your business grows, you'll need to build a team that can support your vision and help you achieve your goals. This means hiring the right people with the right skills and experience, and creating a positive and productive work culture.

6. Analyze Your Finances: As you grow your business, it's important to keep a close eye on your finances. This includes analyzing your cash flow, expenses, and revenue, and making adjustments as needed. Use financial reports and data to make informed decisions about investments, expenses, and growth opportunities.

7. Seek Out Opportunities for Growth: Finally, look for opportunities to grow your business. This can include expanding into new markets, partnering with other businesses, or investing in new technologies or equipment. Keep an open mind and stay on the lookout for opportunities that align with your business goals and values.

Growing a successful business takes time and effort, but it's worth it in the end. By following these key steps, you can build a thriving business that generates wealth and success for years to come.

Mindful Spending

The importance of mindful spending

When it comes to managing finances, it's easy to focus on earning more money or finding ways to save. While those are important aspects, it's equally important to cultivate a habit of mindful spending. Mindful spending means making intentional, conscious decisions about how you spend your money, rather than simply letting it slip away without thought.

One of the key benefits of mindful spending is that it helps you align your spending with your values and goals. When you take the time to reflect on what truly matters to you, you can then make purchasing decisions that are in line with those values. This not only gives your spending more purpose, but it can also lead to greater satisfaction and fulfillment in your life.

Another advantage of mindful spending is that it helps you avoid impulse purchases and buyer's remorse. By taking a step back and considering the long-term impact of a purchase, you can make a more informed decision and avoid the regret that often comes with buying something on a whim.

To cultivate mindful spending, it's important to start with awareness. Take time to track your spending, so you can see where your money is going and identify areas where you might be overspending or spending on things that don't align with your values. From there, you can start to set priorities and create a budget that reflects your values and goals.

It's also important to recognize the role that emotions play in our spending habits. Sometimes we buy things to fill an emotional void or to boost our mood, rather than because we actually need or value the item. By becoming more mindful of these emotional triggers, you can start to make more intentional choices about your spending.

Finally, it's worth noting that mindful spending doesn't mean depriving yourself of all luxuries or pleasures. It's simply about being intentional and conscious about how you spend your money, so that you can get the most value and enjoyment out of every dollar. By focusing on what truly matters to you and making choices that align with your values and goals, you can create a more fulfilling and satisfying financial life.

Practical tips for mindful spending

Mindful spending is an essential aspect of managing your finances effectively. It involves being aware of where your money goes and making intentional decisions about how you spend it. By practicing mindful spending, you can gain control over your finances, prioritize your values and goals, and make informed choices that align with your financial objectives.

Here are some practical tips for practicing mindful spending:

1. Track your expenses: The first step to mindful spending is to understand where your money is going. Keep a record of all your expenses, including small purchases such as coffee or snacks, and categorize them based on the type of expense. You

can use apps or spreadsheets to make it easier to track your spending.

2. Set a budget: Based on your expenses, create a realistic budget that aligns with your financial goals. Identify your fixed expenses, such as rent, bills, and debt payments, and allocate a portion of your income towards savings and investments. Having a budget can help you stay on track and avoid overspending.

3. Prioritize your spending: Before making a purchase, ask yourself if it aligns with your financial priorities and goals. If the answer is no, consider holding off on the purchase or finding a more affordable alternative. For example, if your goal is to save for a down payment on a house, you may need to cut back on discretionary expenses such as dining out or buying new clothes.

4. Avoid impulse buying: Impulse purchases can quickly add up and derail your financial plan. When you feel the urge to buy something, take a step back and think about whether it's something you really need or want. Consider waiting a day or two before making the purchase to see if you still feel the same way.

5. Practice mindful consumption: Mindful spending is not just about what you buy but also about how you consume. Consider the impact of your purchases on the environment and society. Choose products that are ethically sourced, sustainable, and align with your values.

6. Shop around: Before making a purchase, compare prices and look for deals and discounts. You can use online tools and apps to help you find the best deals on products and services.

7. Use cash: Studies have shown that people tend to spend less when using cash compared to credit cards or other forms of payment. Consider using cash for discretionary expenses or setting a limit on your credit card spending.

In summary, practicing mindful spending involves being intentional and deliberate about how you spend your money. By tracking your expenses, setting a budget, prioritizing your spending, avoiding impulse buying, practicing mindful consumption, shopping around, and using cash, you can gain control over your finances and achieve your financial goals.

Creating a spending plan

Creating a spending plan is a crucial step towards financial success. A spending plan, also known as a budget, is a detailed breakdown of your income and expenses. It helps you keep track of your spending habits and make necessary adjustments to achieve your financial goals.

To create a spending plan, the first step is to determine your income. This includes any regular paychecks, freelance work, or any other sources of income. Once you have calculated your total income, you can move on to creating categories for your expenses.

It is important to be thorough when creating categories for your expenses. The more detailed your categories, the easier it will be to track your spending habits. Categories may include rent/mortgage, utilities, transportation, groceries, entertainment, debt payments, and savings.

After categorizing your expenses, it is important to assign a realistic amount to each category based on your spending habits. Be sure to factor in any irregular expenses, such as car repairs or medical bills, and allocate a portion of your income towards savings or investments.

Once you have assigned a dollar amount to each category, you can then begin tracking your spending. There are a variety of tools available, such as spreadsheets or budgeting apps, that can help you track your spending and ensure that you are staying within your budget.

It is important to review and adjust your spending plan regularly. Life changes, and so do our spending habits. By reviewing your spending plan on a regular basis, you can identify areas where you may need to cut back or areas where you can allocate more funds.

Creating a spending plan may seem daunting at first, but it is an essential tool for achieving financial stability and success. By taking the time to create a detailed spending plan and consistently tracking your spending, you can make the necessary adjustments to reach your financial goals.

Financial Independence

<u>Defining financial independence</u>

Financial independence can mean different things to different people, but at its core, it refers to the ability to sustain your desired lifestyle without being dependent on a paycheck or an outside source of income. Achieving financial independence is a major goal for many people because it provides a sense of security, flexibility, and freedom. It means being in control of your finances and your life, and having the ability to make choices based on your values and priorities, rather than being limited by financial constraints.

Financial independence is often associated with retirement, but it doesn't necessarily mean that you have to stop working altogether. It's more about having the choice to work or not work, and being able to pursue activities and passions that align with your values and interests, without being bound by financial obligations.

Financial independence is not an overnight accomplishment, but rather a journey that requires planning, discipline, and patience. It typically involves setting financial goals, reducing expenses, increasing income, investing wisely, and building a financial safety net.

For many people, financial independence is a process that begins with financial stability. This means having enough savings and assets to cover your basic needs and unexpected expenses, such as a medical emergency or a car repair. Once you have achieved financial stability, you can focus on building wealth and creating passive income streams that can provide long-term financial security.

Ultimately, financial independence means having the freedom and flexibility to design a life that aligns with your values and priorities, and being able to enjoy the fruits of your labor without financial stress or worries. While it may require sacrifice and hard work in the short term, the benefits of achieving financial independence are priceless and can lead to a more fulfilling and rewarding life.

Steps to achieve financial independence

Achieving financial independence is a long-term goal that requires discipline, dedication, and a solid plan. While everyone's path to financial independence may differ, there are some key steps that can help you get there.

1. Set clear goals: Define what financial independence means to you and establish specific, measurable, achievable, relevant, and time-bound (SMART) goals to help you get there. This may include reaching a certain amount of savings, eliminating debt, or generating enough passive income to cover your expenses.
2. Create a budget: Develop a budget that aligns with your financial goals and helps you prioritize your spending. This can help you identify areas where you can cut back on expenses and redirect those funds toward your savings and investments.
3. Reduce debt: Eliminating debt can free up more of your income to invest and save toward financial independence. Consider creating a debt repayment

plan and focusing on paying off high-interest debt first.

4. Build an emergency fund: Having a cushion of savings can help protect you from unexpected expenses or job loss. Aim to save at least six months of living expenses in an emergency fund.

5. Invest early and often: Starting to invest early can help you take advantage of compound interest, which can significantly increase your returns over time.

6. Build a diversified portfolio: Diversifying your investments can help minimize risk and maximize returns. Consider investing in a mix of stocks, bonds, and real estate to build a well-rounded portfolio.

7. Increase your income: Finding ways to increase your income, whether through a side hustle, a higher paying job, or passive income streams, can help you reach your financial goals faster.

8. Live below your means: While it can be tempting to increase your spending as your income grows, living below your means can help you save more money and invest more toward financial independence.

9. Stay the course: Achieving financial independence takes time, and it's important to stay committed to your goals even when faced with setbacks or challenges. Regularly review your progress and adjust your plan as needed.

By following these steps, you can set yourself up for long-term financial success and achieve financial independence. Remember, the journey to financial independence may not be easy, but the rewards are well worth the effort.

Benefits of financial independence

Financial independence is a term that is often associated with achieving personal financial goals and freedom. It is a state where an individual has enough resources to support their desired lifestyle without the need for full-time work or dependence on others. While the concept of financial independence may seem daunting or unattainable to some, it is achievable through consistent effort and financial discipline.

One of the most significant benefits of financial independence is the freedom it provides. It allows individuals to pursue their passions, spend time with their loved ones, and engage in activities that bring them joy. Financial independence also provides a sense of security and peace of mind, knowing that one has the means to handle unexpected expenses and emergencies.

Another benefit of financial independence is the ability to retire comfortably. With financial independence, individuals can retire earlier and enjoy a more relaxed lifestyle. They do not have to worry about working full-time until their retirement age or relying solely on their pension or social security benefits.

Additionally, financial independence allows individuals to pursue their dreams and take calculated risks. It provides them with the opportunity to start a business, travel the world, or pursue education without the burden of financial stress. They can invest their time and resources in endeavors they are passionate about without worrying about financial instability.

Moreover, achieving financial independence can set a positive example for future generations. It teaches the value of hard work, financial discipline, and strategic planning. It can motivate and inspire others to pursue their financial goals and achieve their own financial independence.

In summary, the benefits of financial independence are numerous and extend beyond just financial freedom. It provides individuals with the opportunity to live their lives on their own terms, retire comfortably, pursue their dreams, and inspire others. Achieving financial independence requires dedication, patience, and financial discipline, but the rewards are well worth the effort.

Protecting Your Wealth

<u>Importance of wealth protection</u>

Wealth protection is a critical aspect of personal finance that is often overlooked. It is essential to ensure that your wealth is safeguarded against risks and uncertainties that may arise. There are various reasons why wealth protection is important.

Firstly, wealth protection helps you to preserve your hard-earned assets. Without proper protection, your assets may be at risk of being lost due to unexpected events such as accidents, lawsuits, or natural disasters. Wealth protection helps to mitigate these risks and ensure that your assets remain intact.

Secondly, wealth protection provides financial security for you and your family. In the event of your untimely death or disability, your assets can be used to support your loved ones. By protecting your wealth, you can ensure that your family's financial future is secure.

Thirdly, wealth protection helps to minimize taxes and other financial obligations. By structuring your assets in a way that minimizes tax liability, you can ensure that you keep more of your wealth. Additionally, proper wealth protection can help you to avoid unnecessary expenses such as probate fees and other legal costs.

There are several strategies that can be used to protect your wealth. One of the most common strategies is insurance. Insurance can help protect your assets against risks such as theft, fire, natural disasters, and accidents. Other strategies may include setting up trusts, creating a will, and incorporating your business.

It is also important to regularly review your wealth protection strategies to ensure that they are still effective. Changes in your personal circumstances, such as marriage, divorce, or the birth of a child, may require adjustments to your wealth protection plan.

Types of insurance

Insurance is a crucial tool for wealth protection, providing a safety net in case of unexpected events. There are several types of insurance available, each serving a different purpose. Let's take a closer look at the most common types of insurance.

1. Life insurance: Life insurance provides financial support to the beneficiaries of the policyholder in the event of their death. The policyholder pays a premium in exchange for coverage, and the beneficiaries receive a lump sum payment or a series of payments known as a death benefit. Life insurance can help cover funeral expenses, pay off outstanding debts, or provide ongoing support for loved ones.

2. Health insurance: Health insurance covers the cost of medical expenses and treatments for the policyholder. This includes doctor's visits, hospital stays, prescription drugs, and other medical services. Health insurance can be obtained through an employer or purchased independently, and there are various types of plans available, including HMOs, PPOs, and high-deductible plans.

3. Auto insurance: Auto insurance provides financial protection in the event of an accident, theft, or damage to a vehicle. There are several types of auto insurance, including liability insurance, collision insurance, and comprehensive insurance. Liability insurance is required by law in most states and covers damages or injuries to other people or property caused by the policyholder. Collision insurance covers damages to the policyholder's vehicle in the event of an accident, while comprehensive insurance covers damages from non-collision events such as theft, vandalism, or natural disasters.

4. Homeowners insurance: Homeowners insurance protects against damage to a home or its contents, as well as liability for injuries or damages caused by the policyholder or their property. This includes coverage for damages caused by fire, theft, natural disasters, and other events. Homeowners insurance can also cover personal property and additional living expenses in the event of a covered loss.

5. Disability insurance: Disability insurance provides income replacement in the event that the policyholder is unable to work due to a disability or illness. Disability insurance can be purchased through an employer or independently, and there are two types of policies available: short-term disability insurance and long-term disability insurance.

6. Long-term care insurance: Long-term care insurance provides coverage for the costs associated with long-term care, such as nursing home care, home health care, and assisted living facilities. Long-term care insurance can help protect against the financial burden of these services, which can be extremely costly.

Overall, insurance is a crucial tool for protecting wealth and mitigating financial risks. It's important to carefully consider the types of insurance needed for personal circumstances and to choose policies with appropriate coverage levels and deductibles.

Creating a comprehensive protection plan

Creating a comprehensive protection plan is an essential step towards securing your financial future. It involves assessing potential risks and identifying the best strategies to mitigate them. Protection planning includes various types of insurance, such as life insurance, health insurance, disability insurance, and property insurance. By creating a plan that addresses your unique needs and circumstances, you can protect your assets, minimize financial losses, and ensure that you and your family are prepared for unexpected events.

The first step in creating a comprehensive protection plan is to assess your potential risks. Consider the various areas of your life that could be impacted by unexpected events, such as accidents, illnesses, or natural disasters. For example, if you own a home, you'll want to consider property insurance to protect against damage caused by weather, theft, or other events. If you have dependents, life insurance can provide financial security for your loved ones in the event of your unexpected death. Additionally, if you have a job that depends on your ability to work, disability insurance can help replace your income if you become unable to work due to injury or illness.

Once you've identified potential risks, the next step is to determine the appropriate types and levels of insurance coverage. Each type of insurance has its own unique features and benefits, so it's important to carefully consider your options and choose the policies that best meet your needs. For example, life insurance policies come in various types, such as term life and permanent life insurance, and each has its own advantages and disadvantages. Health insurance policies can have different levels of coverage, deductibles, and out-of-pocket maximums, so it's important to understand the details of each plan.

It's also important to consider the costs associated with each type of insurance coverage. While insurance can provide valuable protection, it can also be expensive. By comparing rates and coverage options from multiple providers, you can find the policies that provide the best value for your money. In some cases, bundling multiple types of insurance with the same provider can also result in cost savings. In addition to insurance, there are other strategies you can use to protect your assets and minimize financial risk. For example, creating an emergency fund can help you cover unexpected expenses without having to rely on credit cards or loans. A will or trust can ensure that your assets are distributed according to your wishes in the event of your death. Regularly reviewing and updating your protection plan can also help ensure that it remains relevant and effective as your circumstances change.

In summary, creating a comprehensive protection plan is an important step towards achieving financial security. By assessing your potential risks, identifying the appropriate types and levels of insurance coverage, and implementing additional strategies to protect your assets, you can minimize financial losses and ensure that you and your family are prepared for unexpected events.

Maintaining Wealth

Strategies for maintaining wealth

Maintaining wealth can be just as challenging as acquiring it. Even after achieving financial independence, it is important to take steps to preserve and grow your wealth. In this subchapter, we will discuss some strategies for maintaining wealth over the long term.

1. Continuously educate yourself: The financial world is constantly changing, and new investment opportunities, tax laws, and economic conditions can all impact your wealth. It is important to stay informed and up-to-date on the latest financial news and trends. Read financial books, attend seminars and workshops, and consult with financial professionals to ensure that you are making informed decisions.

2. Diversify your investments: A diversified portfolio can help protect your wealth against market fluctuations and unexpected events. Invest in a mix of asset classes such as stocks, bonds, and real estate, and spread your investments across different sectors and regions. Rebalance your portfolio periodically to ensure that your asset allocation remains aligned with your goals and risk tolerance.

3. Minimize taxes: Taxes can significantly reduce your investment returns and erode your wealth over time. Make sure you are taking advantage of all available tax deductions and credits, such as retirement account contributions, charitable donations, and investment expenses. Consider working with a tax professional to minimize your tax liabilities and ensure compliance with all tax laws.

4. Plan for the unexpected: Unforeseen events such as illness, disability, or death can quickly deplete your wealth if you are not prepared. Consider purchasing insurance policies such as disability, life, and long-term care insurance to protect against these risks. Keep an emergency fund in cash or other liquid assets to cover unexpected expenses.

5. Avoid debt: High levels of debt can be a major obstacle to maintaining wealth over the long term. Avoid taking on high-interest debt such as credit card balances and car loans, and prioritize paying off any outstanding debts. Consider working with a financial planner to develop a debt repayment plan that aligns with your goals.

6. Control expenses: Even small expenses can add up over time and reduce your wealth. Review your spending habits regularly and look for opportunities to cut unnecessary expenses. Consider negotiating bills and fees, using coupons and discount codes, and making bulk purchases to save money.

7. Practice good financial habits: Good financial habits can help you maintain wealth over the long term. These include setting financial goals, living within your means, saving regularly, and tracking your expenses. Consider working with a financial planner to develop a comprehensive financial plan that takes into account your current situation and future goals.

In conclusion, maintaining wealth requires ongoing effort and attention. By continuously educating yourself, diversifying your investments, minimizing taxes, planning for the unexpected, avoiding debt, controlling expenses, and practicing good financial habits, you can help ensure the long-term preservation and growth of your wealth.

Avoiding Common Financial Pitfalls

Managing your finances can be challenging, especially when you're just starting out or going through a major life change. It's easy to make mistakes that can have long-term consequences. However, with a little planning and some simple strategies, you can avoid many of the common financial pitfalls that people often encounter.

1. Not having a budget: One of the biggest mistakes people make is not having a budget. Without a budget, it's easy to overspend and get into debt. Creating a budget allows you to see exactly how much money you have coming in and going out each month. This can help you identify areas where you can cut back and save more money.
2. Living beyond your means: It's important to live within your means. This means not spending more than you earn. If you're constantly living beyond your means, you'll likely accumulate debt and struggle to make ends meet. Instead, try to find ways to reduce your expenses and increase your income.
3. Failing to save for emergencies: Life is unpredictable, and emergencies can happen at any time. If you don't have money set aside for emergencies, you may find yourself in a difficult financial situation. Aim to save at least three to six months' worth of living expenses in an emergency fund.
4. Ignoring debt: It's easy to ignore debt and hope it will go away, but that's not a viable strategy. If you have debt, create a plan to pay it off as soon as

possible. This may involve cutting back on expenses, increasing your income, or seeking help from a financial advisor.

5. Not investing for the future: Investing can be a great way to grow your wealth over time, but many people fail to invest for the future. This can leave you with inadequate savings for retirement or other long-term goals. Talk to a financial advisor about the best investment strategies for your situation.

6. Not having insurance: Insurance can protect you and your assets in case of an unexpected event. This includes health insurance, auto insurance, home insurance, and life insurance. Make sure you have adequate coverage for your needs.

7. Making emotional financial decisions: It's easy to make financial decisions based on emotions, but this can lead to costly mistakes. Avoid making impulsive decisions and take the time to think through your options before making any major financial decisions.

8. Failing to plan for the future: Finally, failing to plan for the future can be a big financial mistake. It's important to have a plan in place for your financial goals, whether it's saving for retirement, buying a home, or starting a business. This can help you stay on track and avoid common financial pitfalls.

In conclusion, by avoiding these common financial mistakes, you can set yourself up for financial success. Creating a budget, living within your means, saving for emergencies, paying off debt, investing for the future, having insurance, making rational decisions, and planning for the future are all essential steps to take in managing your finances. With some discipline and perseverance, you can achieve your financial goals and enjoy a more secure financial future.

Creating a Legacy

Building wealth is not just about achieving financial security in the present; it is also about securing the future for yourself and your loved ones. Creating a legacy that will outlast you is an important part of personal finance. A legacy can mean different things to different people, but it generally refers to the positive impact you leave on the world, whether it's through your philanthropic work or the financial security you provide for future generations.

One of the most important aspects of creating a legacy is estate planning. Estate planning involves creating a plan for what will happen to your assets after you pass away. This can include creating a will, establishing a trust, and designating beneficiaries for your retirement accounts and life insurance policies.

In addition to estate planning, there are other ways to create a lasting legacy. One way is to establish a philanthropic foundation or donate to charitable organizations. This can involve donating money, volunteering time, or using your skills and expertise to help others. Not only does philanthropy allow you to make a positive impact on the world, but it can also provide a sense of purpose and fulfillment in your life.

Another way to create a legacy is to pass on your values and knowledge to future generations. This can involve teaching your children and grandchildren about personal finance, entrepreneurship, and the importance of giving back. By instilling these values in your loved ones, you can ensure that your legacy lives on through their actions and the impact they make on the world.

Finally, creating a legacy can also mean leaving a positive impact on the environment. This can involve supporting environmentally friendly initiatives and investing in companies that prioritize sustainability. By taking care of the planet, you can help create a better world for future generations.

In conclusion, creating a legacy is an important part of personal finance. By engaging in estate planning, philanthropy, passing on your values and knowledge, and supporting environmental initiatives, you can leave a lasting impact on the world. Start thinking about how you can create a legacy today, and take steps to ensure that your impact will be felt for generations to come.

Conclusion: The Art of Wealth

<u>Recap of key concepts</u>

In this guide, we have covered a wide range of financial concepts, strategies, and practices aimed at helping you achieve long-term financial success. It's important to recap some of the key concepts we have discussed to ensure that you have a solid understanding of the main ideas.

First, we talked about the importance of setting financial goals, which involves identifying your priorities and creating a plan to achieve them. This step is essential because it helps you stay motivated and focused on your long-term financial objectives.

We also discussed the concept of budgeting, which involves creating a detailed plan for managing your income and expenses. By creating a budget, you can track your spending and identify areas where you can cut back, which will help you save money and achieve your financial goals faster.

Another important concept we covered is the different types of passive income, including rental properties, dividend stocks, and online businesses. Creating multiple streams of passive income can help you generate consistent cash flow and build long-term wealth.

In addition, we explored the benefits of real estate investing, including the potential for appreciation and the ability to generate rental income. We also discussed different types of real estate investments, such as single-family homes, multi-family properties, and commercial real estate.

To help you become a successful entrepreneur, we provided tips for starting and growing a business, including conducting market research, creating a business plan, and building a strong team.

We also emphasized the importance of mindful spending and provided practical tips for creating a spending plan and sticking to it. This step is crucial for achieving financial independence and building long-term wealth.

To achieve financial independence, we outlined steps such as paying off debt, building an emergency fund, and investing for the future. By following these steps, you can create a solid financial foundation and achieve financial freedom.

In addition, we discussed the importance of wealth protection, including different types of insurance and creating a comprehensive protection plan. This step is critical for safeguarding your financial assets and ensuring that you and your loved ones are protected in the event of unexpected events.

To maintain wealth, we provided strategies such as diversifying your investments, continuing to learn about personal finance, and avoiding common financial pitfalls.

Finally, we discussed creating a legacy, which involves passing on your wealth to future generations and giving back to your community. By following these steps, you can create a lasting financial legacy that will benefit your loved ones and the world around you.

Overall, the key concepts we have covered in this guide can help you achieve financial success and create a secure financial future for yourself and your family. Remember to stay focused, stay disciplined, and continue to learn and grow in your personal finance journey.

Final thoughts on minimalist wealth-building

As we come to the end of this guide on minimalist wealth-building, it's important to reflect on the key concepts and takeaways that we have discussed.

We have explored the idea that building wealth doesn't have to involve complicated strategies or sacrificing the things we love. Instead, it's about adopting a mindset of intentional living, where we focus on the things that truly matter and learn to make the most of what we have.

Throughout this guide, we have examined a variety of approaches and techniques that can help us build wealth while staying true to our minimalist principles. We've discussed the benefits of real estate investing, entrepreneurship, and mindful spending, as well as strategies for achieving financial independence and protecting our wealth.

Ultimately, the key to minimalist wealth-building is finding a balance between our desire for financial security and our commitment to living simply and intentionally. By taking a thoughtful and intentional approach to our finances, we can create a legacy that reflects our values and goals, while also ensuring that we are able to live a life of abundance and meaning.

It's worth noting that building wealth is not an overnight process, and there may be setbacks and challenges along the way. However, by staying focused on our goals, staying true to our values, and being willing to adapt and learn, we can achieve financial independence and create the life that we want for ourselves and our loved ones.

Thank you for taking the time to read this guide on minimalist wealth-building. I hope that you found it informative, insightful, and inspiring.

At its core, this guide is about empowering you to take control of your finances and pursue financial freedom through mindful spending, intentional saving, and strategic investing. I believe that these principles are essential for anyone looking to build lasting wealth and create a more fulfilling life.

If you found this guide helpful, I would be grateful if you could leave a positive review. Your feedback is invaluable to me, and it helps me to continue creating high-quality content that meets your needs and exceeds your expectations.

Thank you again for your time and attention. I wish you all the best on your journey towards financial freedom, and I look forward to hearing from you soon.